A Flower is a Friend

Frieda Wishinsky

ILLUSTRATIONS BY

Karen Patkau

pajamapress

First published in Canada and the United States in 2023

www.pajamapress.ca   info@pajamapress.ca

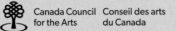
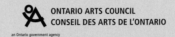

The publisher gratefully acknowledges the support of the Canada Council for the Arts and the Ontario Arts Council for its publishing program. We acknowledge the financial support of the Government of Canada through the Canada Book Fund (CBF) for our publishing activities.

Library and Archives Canada Cataloguing in Publication
Title: A flower is a friend / Frieda Wishinsky ; illustrations by Karen Patkau.
Names: Wishinsky, Frieda, author. | Patkau, Karen, illustrator.
Description: Includes index.
Identifiers: Canadiana 20220466246 | ISBN 9781772782806 (hardcover)
Subjects: LCSH: Flowers—Juvenile literature. | LCSH: Flowers—Pictorial works—Juvenile literature.
Classification: LCC SB406.5 .W57 2023 | DDC j635.9—dc23

Publisher Cataloging-in-Publication Data (U.S.)

Names: Wishinsky, Frieda, author. | Patkau, Karen, illustrator.
Title: A Flower Is a Friend / Frieda Wishinsky ; illustrations by Karen Patkau.
Description: Toronto, Ontario Canada : Pajama Press, 2022. | Includes index. | Summary: Brief, lyrical text names the roles flowers play in a garden ecosystem, providing food and shelter and interacting with rain, wind, and light. Bright, close-up illustrations showcase blossoms and the creatures who visit them, including insects, hummingbirds, a mouse, and a frog. Questions on each spread prompt readers to think about the relationships between the flowers and creatures, and information about those relationships is shared in spotlight paragraphs about each creature in the back matter. Includes an index of flowers." -- Provided by publisher.
Identifiers: ISBN 978-1-77278-280-6 (hardcover)
Subjects: LCSH: Flower gardening - Juvenile literature. | Gardening to attract wildlife - Juvenile literature. | Garden ecology - Juvenile literature. | BISAC: JUVENILE NONFICTION / Science & Nature / Flowers & Plants. | JUVENILE NONFICTION / Gardening. | JUVENILE NONFICTION / Animals / Butterflies, Moths & Caterpillars.
Classification: LCC QH541.5.G37 | DDC 577.554 - dc23

Original art created digitally
Cover and book design—Lorena González Guillén
Magnifying glass courtesy of veectezy.com

Manufactured in China by WKT Company

Pajama Press Inc.
11 Davies Avenue, Suite 103, Toronto, Ontario Canada, M4M 2A9

Distributed in Canada by UTP Distribution
5201 Dufferin Street Toronto, Ontario Canada, M3H 5T8

Distributed in the U.S. by Ingram Publisher Services
1 Ingram Blvd. La Vergne, TN 37086, USA

To Gracie, who makes me smile
every day, and to Karen Patkau,
who helped transform our love
of gardens into a beautiful book

—F.W.

To my mother, who loves nature,
and to Frieda, whose garden
inspired this book

—K.P.

We are flowers! We grow.
We bloom.
We help our friends.
Our friends help us.
We...

Why are ladybugs and flowers friends?

Wake to the sunlight

Why would a morning glory
be happy to see a dragonfly?

Feed a hummingbird

What attracts a hummingbird
to a honeysuckle?

Dust a bumblebee

While visiting a flower like a black-eyed Susan,
where does a bee collect pollen?

Burst with color

How is a gecko
a friend to a bird of paradise?

Kiss a butterfly

Why do butterflies and
zinnias love being together?

Drink the rain

How does the rain
help cornflowers and snails?

Shade a frog

Why does a frog
like sitting under a waterlily?

Dance with the wind

What draws a beetle
to a magnolia?

21

Hide a mouse

Why would a mouse
sleep in a tulip?

Spread our perfume

How could a spider
help the Queen of the Night flower?

And close at night.

While a crocus closes for the night,
what does a bat do?

Flowers have all sorts of friends.
Can you find them?

Why are flowers and creatures friends?

Many plants and animals depend on each other to survive and grow.

Insects and animals drink the sweet **nectar** found in flowers. As they do, they spread the plant's **pollen**, which helps the plant make seeds.

Some creatures gather seeds to eat. After they bury or scatter them, new flowers grow. Creatures also help by eating insects like aphids and gnats that nibble on flowers.

Ladybugs: When ladybugs eat their favorite pollen and nectar from plants such as daisies, yarrow, and marigolds, they also snack on pesky aphids. Aphids suck the juice from the stems, leaves, and buds of flowers. Ladybugs move around the garden and pollinate flowers too.

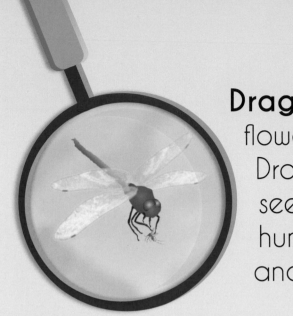

Dragonflies: Dragonflies have been flower helpers since dinosaur times. Dragonflies use their large eyes to see everywhere at once and catch hundreds of insects like mosquitoes and gnats.

Hummingbirds: Hummingbirds are attracted to bright, tube-shaped flowers like honeysuckle.
The hummingbird's long beak and tongue help it suck the flower's nectar. While it drinks in the nectar, pollen sticks to the hummingbird's body. A hungry hummingbird might pollinate over 1000 flowers a day.

Bumblebees: As a bumblebee sips nectar from a flower, it collects pollen on its hairy back legs. When it flies off, it pollinates other flowers, especially wildflowers. Bumblebees can fly in cooler temperatures than other bees, so they can pollinate flowers that bloom early in the spring.

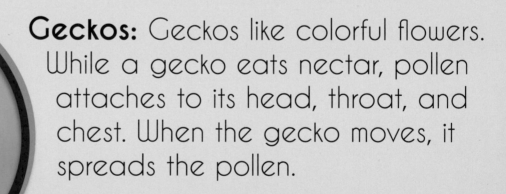

Geckos: Geckos like colorful flowers. While a gecko eats nectar, pollen attaches to its head, throat, and chest. When the gecko moves, it spreads the pollen.

Butterflies: Butterflies love sipping the nectar of bright flowers. While they drink, pollen sticks to their bodies. Before a butterfly takes off to sip more nectar and pollinate new flowers it shakes or shivers. That helps raise its temperature so it can fly easily.

Snails: Snails and flowers both need the moisture from rain to live. Snails come out after a rain. They are good climbers and travel by releasing slime and gliding over it. Although snails chew new leaves and flowers, they also help clean the garden by eating dead plant material.

Frogs: While frogs enjoy the shade of a waterlily, they gobble up insects harmful to plants. They also lay their eggs under lily pads. Frogs often dip in water to keep their bodies moist, which helps them breathe. They drink water through a **drinking patch** on their skin.

Beetles: For millions of years beetles have been drawn to the spicy scent of magnolias. Beetles crawl around the wide-open flower with its tough skin, nibble its pollen, and spread it around.

Mice: Sometimes after a harvest mouse has snacked on a tulip's pollen, it falls asleep inside the flower. Some mice help flowers by spreading pollen that attaches to their bodies.

Spiders: Garden spiders help flowers by eating insects like aphids and flies that chew on flowers and may spread disease. The garden spider spins a sticky web to capture the insects.

Bats: Nectar-eating bats can fly at night and pollinate more than 500 types of plants. They can carry pollen even farther than bees. Fruit-eating bats help new trees in hot tropical areas grow by dropping seeds. Insect-eating bats eat bugs that harm plants and bother gardeners!

Index of Flowers